Don R. Caffery

Our Holy Father, the Pope

The Papacy from Saint Peter to the Present

Illustrations: Emmanuel Beaudesson

MAGNIFICAT® • **Ignatius**

Acknowledgments—
I would like to thank my wife, Jo Lynn, for being my loving audience and friendly critic. Thanks to my children, Ralph and Mary, for their love and patience during the writing of the book. Thanks to the late Professor Robert J. Edgeworth of Louisiana State University, for his help with translation and pronunciation of Latin terms. Thanks to Mr. Stephen K. Ray for his invaluable materials on the Papacy, including the book *Upon This Rock*, and the video *Footprints of God: Peter*. Special thanks to Mr. James Louviere of Champions of the Truth, for permission to use his song title *Simon the Rock*, and for being my most constant friend and source of encouragement.

Nihil Obstat: Very Reverend Than N. Vu
             Vicar General
Imprimatur: ✠ Robert W. Muench
             Bishop of Baton Rouge
             July 26, 2013

Under the direction of Romain Lizé, Vice President, Magnificat

Editor, Magnificat: Isabelle Galmiche
Editor, Ignatius: Vivian Dudro
Assistant of the Editor: Pascale Vandewalle
Layout Designer: Élise Borel
Production: Thierry Dubus, Sabine Marioni

Contents

Our Holy Father, the Pope

We are in a crowd at a sports stadium today.
Thousands of people are here!
Suddenly a roar goes up.
A car drives into the stadium.
A man gets out, all dressed in white.
He blesses the crowd with the Sign of the Cross.
Hooray! It is our Holy Father, the Pope!

But what is a Pope?
And why do we need one anyway?

Let's find out.
We will go back to the time of Jesus.
We will learn about the first Pope.

5

A Man Called Simon

Simon was a fisherman.
He lived in Galilee in the time of Jesus.
He was neither rich nor famous.

But our Lord Jesus knew everything.
He knew that Simon was the kind of man who could lead others.
He knew that, one day, He would make Simon the head of
His Church on earth.

Jesus met Simon by the Sea of Galilee.
Jesus called Simon to follow him, to be His disciple.
And I will make you a fisher of men, Jesus said.

Jesus gave Simon a new name.
In those days, a man's name was very important.
It stood for who he was.
Jesus said, **So you are Simon the son of John?
You shall be called Cephas.**

"Cephas", or "Kepha" (KAY-fah),
means "rock" in the language Jesus spoke.
No one had had that name before!
In English, we say "Peter", from the Latin word for "rock".
That is why we know Simon today as Saint Peter.

Simon on the Sea

One night, Simon Peter was in a boat on the Sea of Galilee. Other disciples of Jesus were in the boat too.

The wind blew.

Waves crashed against the boat.

Then the men saw Jesus coming toward them, walking on the water.

They were afraid.

They did not understand yet that Jesus was God.

Having more courage than the others,

Peter called out to Jesus,

Lord, if it is you, bid me come to you on the water.

Jesus replied, **Come**.

Peter jumped out of the boat and began walking on the water!

But then Peter took his eyes off Jesus.

He looked at the wind upon the waves.

And he was afraid.

Peter began to sink!

He cried out, **Lord, save me**.

Jesus caught him and said,

O you of little faith, why did you doubt?

Peter was like many of us.
Sometimes we begin bravely
but then become afraid.

Jesus loved Peter.
Jesus saved him.
Jesus showed Peter that He would help him
when he was weak.

9

Simon the Rock

One day, Jesus brought His disciples to a special place with a long name: Caesarea Philippi (Says-uh-REE-uh Fil-LIP-eye). Here was a great wall of rock.

Jesus asked His friends, **Who do men say that the Son of man is?** ("Son of man" was one of the names Jesus called himself to show that He was a human being as well as the Son of God.)

The disciples answered that many people thought Jesus was one of the prophets, that is, those sent by God to deliver a special message.

Then Jesus asked, **But who do you say that I am?**

Simon Peter said, **You are the Christ, the Son of the living God.**

And Jesus said, **Blessed are you, Simon, for my Father in heaven has revealed this to you. And I tell you, you are Peter, and on this rock I will build my church.**

Jesus is God, the real Rock of our faith. And He chose Simon Peter to be strong like a rock so that he could lead the Church.

The Keys of the Kingdom

Then Jesus said to Peter,
I will give you the keys of the kingdom
of heaven.

Jesus has the keys of the kingdom of heaven.

In giving us His Church, Jesus gave us the way to heaven.

Giving Peter His keys meant that Jesus gave Peter authority over His Church.

In ages past, a king's most important officer was His royal steward.

The royal steward took care of the king's household.

He carried the great keys of the royal palace.

Whenever the king was away, the steward ruled in his place
until the king returned.

One who rules in the place of another is called a vicar.

Jesus, the King of Kings, chose Peter to be His vicar.

And when Jesus returned to heaven,
Peter looked after His Church.

After Peter died, another man took his place.

For almost two thousand years, the keys of the kingdom
of heaven have been handed down to Peter's successors,
that is, those who have followed him as the vicar of Christ.

The Last Supper

When Jesus knew the time for Him to die on the Cross was near, He gathered His twelve closest disciples for a last meal.

These twelve men were His apostles.
The word "apostle" refers to someone sent on a special mission.
Jesus had already sent the Twelve to teach and heal in His name.
At the Last Supper He gave them another task.

It was the Passover, an important holiday for the Jews.
With a special Passover meal, the Jews recalled
the way God had freed them from slavery in Egypt.

As Jesus and His apostles were at table eating, Jesus took bread.
Giving thanks to God, He blessed the bread,
broke it, and gave it to His apostles saying,
Take this, all of you, and eat
of it, for this is my Body,
which will be given up
for you.

Then He took the chalice of wine.
Giving thanks and blessing the chalice,
He gave it to His apostles saying,
Take this, all of you, and drink from it,
for this is the chalice of my Blood,
the Blood of the new and eternal covenant,
which will be poured out for you and for many
for the forgiveness of sins.
Do this in memory of me.

The Last Supper of Jesus was the first Mass.
Jesus made Peter and the other apostles His priests.
As Jesus commanded, His priests have continued
to celebrate the Mass in memory of Him.

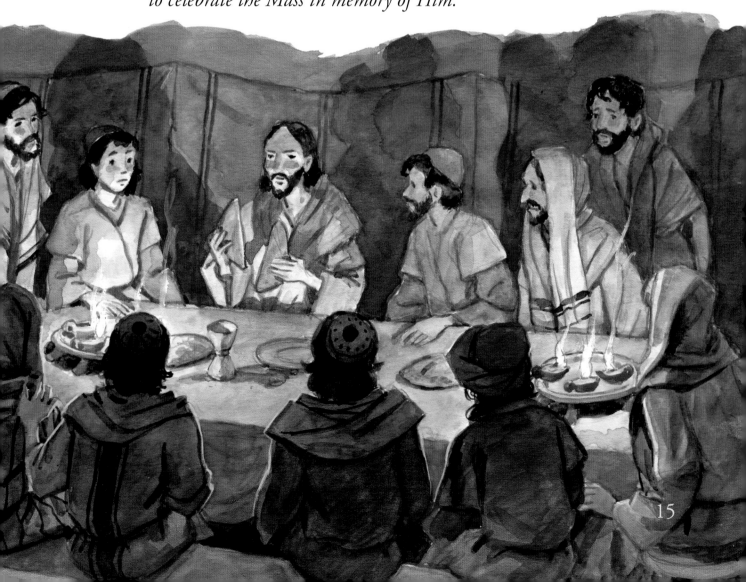

The Cock Crows

That night, after the Last Supper, Jesus was arrested. He was put on trial for claiming to be the Son of God.

Peter waited outside in the courtyard.
 A woman saw Peter and recognized him.
 She said, You also were with Jesus.

 Peter was afraid.
In his weakness,
he failed to put his trust in God.
He said, I do not know what you mean.

 Two more times, he denied knowing Jesus.
 After the third time, a cock crowed.
 Peter remembered what Jesus had told him earlier,
    Before the cock crows,
      you will deny me three times.
    Peter broke down and cried.

Peter was sad because he had denied Jesus.
   He was even sadder when Jesus died on the Cross.
   But on Easter his sorrow was turned into joy.
      Peter was the first apostle to see our risen Savior!

A few days after Jesus rose from the dead,
Peter and some other apostles
went fishing on the Sea of Galilee.
When they neared the shore,
Jesus appeared to them on the beach.
Peter jumped into the water and swam to Jesus!

Later, Jesus said to Peter.
Simon, son of John, do you love me more than these?
Peter answered, **Yes, Lord; you know that I love you.**
Jesus said, **Feed my lambs.**

Again Jesus asked Peter, **Simon, son of John,
do you love me?**
Yes, Lord; you know that I love you.
Jesus said, **Tend my sheep.**

Then Jesus spoke for the third time.
Simon, son of John, do you love me?
Peter felt sad because Jesus asked him a third time.
He remembered how he had denied Jesus three times.
Peter said, **Lord, you know everything;
you know that I love you.**
Jesus said to him, **Feed my sheep.**

Who are the sheep of Jesus?
We are. We who follow Jesus are His sheep.
Jesus is our Good Shepherd.
Jesus chose Peter to be a good shepherd too.

Soon after this, Jesus led His apostles to a hilltop.
He told them to teach and baptize everyone.
Then Jesus ascended into heaven,
that is, He rose into the sky and disappeared.
But He did not leave His flock without a shepherd.
Jesus left us Peter and his successors to watch over His sheep,
until He returns on the last day.

The First Pope

Ten days later came the feast of Pentecost.
On this holiday, Jews celebrated
that God had given Moses
the Ten Commandments.

Peter and the disciples were at prayer.
The Holy Spirit rushed into the room,
like a mighty wind.
The Holy Spirit could be seen,
as tongues of fire,
above each one's head.

The apostles were filled with joy.
They were no longer afraid.
They began proclaiming the good news of Jesus.

A crowd gathered outside the house.
Peter told the people that Jesus was the Christ,
the Son of God, who had risen from the dead.
He told them to be sorry for their sins and be baptized.
About three thousand people joined the Church that day!

*Peter and the other apostles spread the good news
to more and more places.
As leader of the apostles, Saint Peter was the first Pope.
The word "pope" means "father".
Saint Peter was a spiritual father to the first Christians.
Peter visited them in their towns and cities.*

Today the Pope is still a father to Christians everywhere.

Many people call him "Papa".

He travels all over the world to visit us.

We are his children in the Lord Jesus Christ.

The Chair of Saint Peter

The good news of Jesus spread rapidly.
At one point, some men in the town of Antioch (ANT-ee-ock) were spreading false teachings.
This was making Christians disagree with each other.

The apostles met together to discuss the problem.
This meeting was the Council of Jerusalem.
The apostles argued for a while, but then Saint Peter spoke.

Peter explained the true teachings of Jesus.
The apostles became quiet.
They accepted Saint Peter's word as coming from God.

Later, Saint Peter moved from Jerusalem.
He became the first bishop of the Christians in Rome.
The word "bishop" comes from the Greek word
for leader, "episkopos".

Today, a bishop's church is called a cathedral,
from the Latin word "cathedra" for "chair".
Like keys, the chair is a sign of authority.
In the Old Testament, the chair of Moses
stood for his authority to rule God's people.
The Chair of Saint Peter stands for the Pope's authority,
which comes from Jesus Christ.

Other apostles became bishops in other cities.
But Peter remained the leader of the whole Church.
For this reason the Catholic Church honors
the Chair of Saint Peter each year on February 22.

Saint Peter knew he would die for Christ.
He also knew that someone had to take his place as chief shepherd.
He prayed to God.
Then he chose a good man, Saint Linus, to replace him.

There has been an unbroken chain of Popes,
from Saint Peter down to our present Pope.
This is a miracle!
This shows that the Church belongs to God
and that it is protected by Him.

The corrupt Emperor Nero arrested Peter.
He knew Saint Peter was the leader of the Christians
and sentenced him to death.
Peter said that he was not worthy to die
the same way Jesus had.
Thus, Peter was crucified upside down.

Saint Peter was buried on Vatican Hill.
His grave was honored by Christians from the start.
Eventually a great church, Saint Peter's Basilica,
was built over it.

FOUR GREAT POPES

Clement I

Pope Clement is also called Saint Clement of Rome. His name is mentioned in the Bible.
He was made a bishop by Saint Peter himself.
He became the fourth Pope, in the year 91.

Clement wrote a letter to the Christians in Corinth.
There had been a schism (SIZ-em), or break, in the faithful there.
A schism is a terrible thing.
Clement's letter helped bring the Christians back together.
Clement was doing his job as shepherd of the whole Church.

Saint Clement gave his life for Christ as a martyr in the year 100.

His feast day is November 28.

Leo the Great

Imagine a Pope facing Attila the Hun.
The Huns were a tribe of fierce warriors.
Attila was their chief.
He wanted to conquer and plunder the Roman Empire.

It was the year 452.
Roman emperors had become Christian by this time.
But the Roman army was weak.
It could not keep the Huns away.
Everyone was afraid.

Pope Leo trusted in God.
Before Attila reached Rome, Leo went out to meet him.
The men stood face to face.
Pope Leo did not have an army.
But he had the power of the name of Jesus Christ.

Attila the Hun was impressed by the brave Pope.
He went away with his army.
Saint Leo had saved Rome!
He was a good shepherd to his people.

His feast day is November 10.

Pius X

In the early 1900s, few people went to Holy Communion.
Many people only went once a year.
Children could not make their First Communion
until they were teenagers.

But then Giuseppe (juh-SEP-pi) Sarto became Pope.
He knew that Jesus loves us.
He knew that people should be as close to Jesus as possible.
He encouraged Catholics to receive Communion often,
not only every Sunday, but even every day if possible!

Our Lord Jesus loves children very, very much.
Once He said, Let the children come to me.
Thanks to Pope Pius, children may receive Jesus
as soon as they are old enough to understand
that Holy Communion is His Body and Blood.

Saint Pius X is called the Children's Pope.

His feast day is August 21.

John Paul II

John Paul II was the first Pope from Poland.
Before he became Pope, his name was Karol Wojtyla (voy-TEE-wah).
As a bishop, he took part in the Second Vatican Council.
Like the Council of Jerusalem, this Council was meant to help
the shepherds of the Church.

But afterward, many Catholics did not agree about what the Council
had taught.

When he became Pope, John Paul wrote many letters to the whole Church.
He explained what the Council had taught.
He travelled all over the world.
He helped to bring Christians together, and to make peace
in the Church.

John Paul especially loved young people.
In 1984, he held the first World Youth Day.
Perhaps you will be able to attend one day.
Like Jesus, John Paul II often said, **Be not afraid**.
Be not afraid to live, to love, and to follow Jesus!

When he is named a saint, his feast day will be October 22.

What Does the Pope Do Today?

Christ told Saint Peter, *Tend my lambs* and *Feed my sheep*. How does the Holy Father do this today?

The Pope is first of all a priest.
Sometimes he is called the Supreme Pontiff,
which means "highest priest".
Like other priests, the Pope offers Holy Mass.
He feeds us with the Body and Blood of Christ.

Second, the Pope is the bishop of Rome.
Like other bishops, the Pope ordains men as new priests.
But only the Pope may choose new bishops,
the successors of the apostles.

The Pope also tends his lambs by teaching us about God.
Saint Peter wrote letters to the entire Church.
Today the Pope still writes these letters.
They teach Christians how to follow Jesus in today's world.

When a council of all the bishops meets together,
the Pope must approve all its decisions and decrees.
Only the Pope may declare men and women to be saints.

At the Last Supper, Jesus said to Peter,
I have prayed for you that your faith may not fail.
When the Pope, speaking officially
as the chief shepherd of Christians,
defines a teaching on faith or morals,
God, the Holy Spirit, protects him from error.

Where Does the Pope Live?

As we have already seen, Peter, the first Pope, died in Rome. Around the year 325, the first Saint Peter's Basilica

was built over his grave.

It stood for over a thousand years!

Then a new Saint Peter's was built.

Many of the world's greatest artists worked on it.

It is one of the most beautiful churches in the world.[1]

Beside Saint Peter's is the Vatican,

the place where the Pope lives and works.

Both Saint Peter's and the Vatican are in Vatican City,

which is the world's smallest country!

Vatican City has its own flag.

It even has its own army—the Swiss Guards.

The Swiss Guards wear colorful uniforms.

They carry lances and battle-axes,

as soldiers did in ages past.

But the Swiss Guards are real soldiers.

They are there to protect the Pope.

1. Another church in Rome, the Basilica of Saint John Lateran, is the Pope's cathedral.

Who Are the Pope's Helpers?

The Holy Father has a big job.
He must lead the Catholic Church
throughout the world.

The Pope's most important helpers are cardinals.
Cardinals are usually bishops who are chosen by the Pope
to be his special advisors.
In the Vatican, cardinals help govern the Church by
leading the offices of the Curia (CURE-ee-uh).

The bishops, priests and lay people
who also work in the Vatican help the Pope
and cardinals stay in touch with every corner
of the globe.

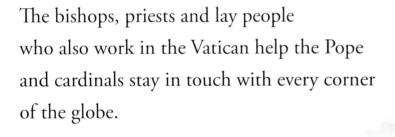

Every day, the Pope receives many letters and telephone calls.
Every day, he meets with many people:
Catholics seeking his encouragement and advice,
leaders of nations who wish to speak with him,
and leaders of other religions too.

There is plenty of ordinary work to be done as well:
keeping Saint Peter's clean, beautiful, and safe for visitors;
helping the Pope with his clothes and meals;
taking care of the Vatican Museums, Library, and Gardens.

How Is a New Pope Chosen?

Saint Peter served as chief shepherd of the Church until he died.
Most of his successors also served for life.
It is possible, though, for a Pope to resign, or step down.
This has happened only a few times in the history of the Church.
Pope Benedict XVI retired in 2013.
He was the first to do this since Pope Gregory XII in 1415.

Thanks to modern media, when the Pope dies or resigns,
the whole world soon knows about it.
The cardinals from all over the world then gather at Saint Peter's Basilica.
They come to mourn for the dead Pope,
if he died in office, and to choose his successor
in a closed meeting called a conclave.

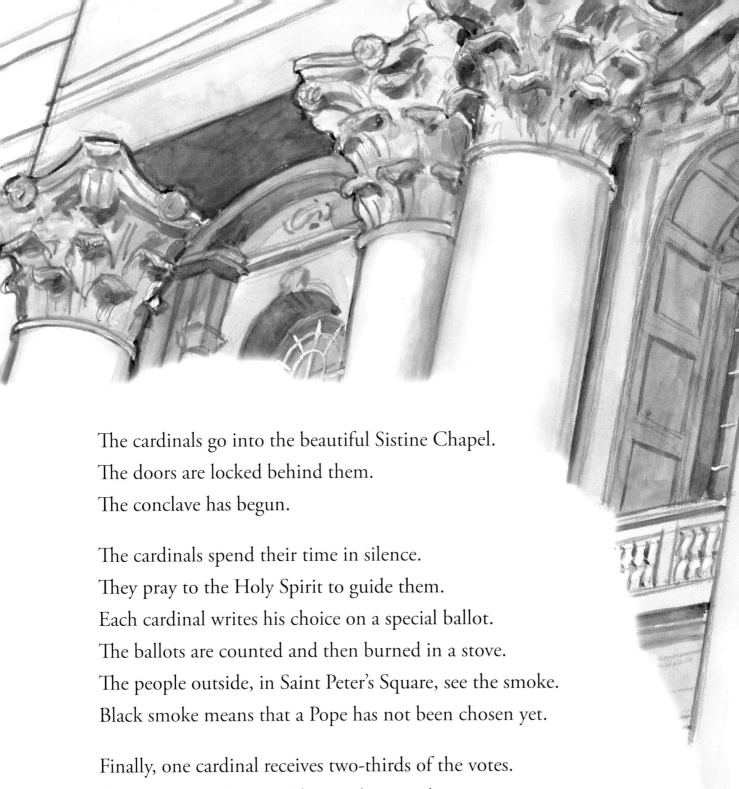

The cardinals go into the beautiful Sistine Chapel.
The doors are locked behind them.
The conclave has begun.

The cardinals spend their time in silence.
They pray to the Holy Spirit to guide them.
Each cardinal writes his choice on a special ballot.
The ballots are counted and then burned in a stove.
The people outside, in Saint Peter's Square, see the smoke.
Black smoke means that a Pope has not been chosen yet.

Finally, one cardinal receives two-thirds of the votes.
The people waiting outside see white smoke.
"Habemus Papam. We have a Pope!"

The new Pope takes a new name.
He puts on the white clothes worn only by the bishop of Rome.
He comes out to the balcony of Saint Peter's.
He speaks to his flock in Rome and to the whole Church for the first time.

Pray for the Holy Father

We have learned about our Holy Father, the Pope.
He is the successor of Saint Peter.
He is the vicar of Christ.
He watches over the entire Catholic Church!

We can help him.
We can love and honor him.
We can listen to him and obey his teaching.

A great saint once said,
Where Peter is, there is the Church.
If we stay with the Pope, we know we are with the true Church.
If we follow the Pope, we know we are following Jesus.

Let us pray for the Holy Father.
Say an Our Father and a Hail Mary every day for his intentions.*
This is how we can help him.
This is one way we can help the Church.

*The Holy Father's prayer intentions can be found at
www.apostleshipofprayer.net.

The Popes
from the Time of Christ to the Present

1. St. Peter (died 67 AD)
2. St. Linus (67– 6)
3. St. Anacletus (76–88)
4. St. Clement I (88–97)
5. St. Evaristus (97–105)
6. St. Alexander I (105–115)
7. St. Sixtus I (115–125)
8. St. Telesphorus (125–136)
9. St. Hyginus (136–140)
10. St. Pius I (140–155)
11. St. Anicetus (155–166)
12. St. Soter (166–175)
13. St. Eleutherius (175–189)
14. St. Victor I (189–199)
15. St. Zephyrinus (199–217)
16. St. Callistus (217–222)
17. St. Urban I (222–230)
18. St. Pontian (230–235)
19. St. Anterus (235–236)
20. St. Fabian (236–250)
21. St. Cornelius (251–253)
22. St. Lucius I (253–254)
23. St. Stephen I (254–257)
24. St. Sixtus II (257–258)
25. St. Dionysius (259–268)
26. St. Felix I (269–274)
27. St. Eutychian (275–283)
28. St. Caius (283–296)
29. St. Marcellinus (296–304)
30. St. Marcellus I (308–309)
31. St. Eusebius (309)
32. St. Melchiades (311–314)
33. St. Sylvester I (314–335)
34. St. Marcus (336)
35. St. Julius I (337–352)
36. Liberius (352–366)
37. St. Damasus I (366–384)
38. St. Siricius (384–399)
39. St. Anastasius I (399–401)
40. St. Innocent I (401–417)
41. St. Zosimus (417–418)
42. St. Boniface I (418–422)
43. St. Celestine I (422–432)
44. St. Sixtus III (432–440)
45. St. Leo I (the Great) (440–461)
46. St. Hilary (461–468)
47. St. Simplicius (468–483)
48. St. Felix III (483–492)
49. St. Gelasius I, 492–496
50. Anastasius II (496–498)
51. St. Symmachus (498–514)
52. St. Hormisdas (514–523)
53. St. John I (523–526)
54. St. Felix IV, 526–530
55. Boniface II (530–532)
56. John II (533–535)
57. St. Agapitus I (535–536)
58. St. Silverius(536–537)
59. Vigilius (537–555)
60. Pelagius I (556–561)
61. John III (561–574)
62. Benedict I (575–579)
63. Pelagius II (579–590)
64. St. Gregory I (the Great) (590–604)
65. Sabinian (604–606)
66. Boniface III (607)
67. St. Boniface IV (608–615)

68. St. Deusdedit (615–618)
69. Boniface V (619–625)
70. Honorius I (625–638)
71. Severinus (640)
72. John IV (640–642)
73. Theodore I (642–649)
74. St. Martin I (649–655)
75. St. Eugene I (654–657)
76. St. Vitalian (657–672)
77. Adeodatus (672–676)
78. Donus (676–678)
79. St. Agatho (678–681)
80. St. Leo II (682–683)
81. St. Benedict II (684–685)
82. John V (685–686)
83. Conon (686–687)
84. St. Sergius I (687–701)
85. John VI (701–705)
86. John VII (705–707)
87. Sisinnius (708)
88. Constantine (708–715)
89. St. Gregory II (715–731)
90. St. Gregory III (731–741)
91. St. Zachary (741–752)
92. Stephen II (752–757)
93. St. Paul I (757–767)
94. Stephen III (768–772)
95. Adrian I (772–795)
96. St. Leo III (795–816)
97. Stephen IV (816–817)
98. St. Paschal I (817–824)
99. Eugene II (824–827)
100. Valentine (827)
101. Gregory IV (827–844)
102. Sergius II (844–847)
103. St. Leo IV (847–855)
104. Benedict III (855–858)
105. St. Nicholas I (the Great) (858–867)
106. Adrian II (867–872)
107. John VIII (872–882)
108. Marinus I (882–884)
109. St. Adrian III (884–885)
110. Stephen V (885–891)
111. Formosus (891–896)
112. Boniface VI (896)
113. Stephen VI (896–897)
114. Romanus (897)
115. Theodore II (897)
116. John IX (898–900)
117. Benedict IV (900–903)
118. Leo V (903)
119. Sergius III (904–911)
120. Anastasius III (911–913)
121. Landus (913–914)
122. John X (914–928)
123. Leo VI (928)
124. Stephen VII (928–931)
125. John XI (931–935)
126. Leo VII (936–939)
127. Stephen VIII (939–942)
128. Marinus II (942–946)
129. Agapitus II (946–955)
130. John XII (955–964)
131. Leo VIII (963–965)
132. Benedict V (964–966)
133. John XIII (965–972)
134. Benedict VI (973–974)

135. Benedict VII (974–983)
136. John XIV (983–984)
137. John XV (985–996)
138. Gregory V (996–999)
139. Sylvester II (999–1003)
140. John XVII (1003)
141. John XVIII (1004–1009)
142. Sergius IV (1009–1012)
143. Benedict VIII (1012–1024)
144. John XIX (1024–1032)
145. Benedict IX (1032–1044)
146. Sylvester III (1045)
147. Benedict IX (1045)
148. Gregory VI (1045–1046)
149. Clement II (1046–1047)
150. Benedict IX (1047–1048)
151. Damasus II (1048)
152. St. Leo IX (1049–1054)
153. Victor II (1055–1057)
154. Stephen IX (1057–1058)
155. Nicholas II (1059–1061)
156. Alexander II (1061–1073)
157. St. Gregory VII (1073–1085)
158. Bl. Victor III (1086–1087)
159. Bl. Urban II (1088–1099)
160. Paschal II (1099–1118)
161. Gelasius II (1118–1119)
162. Callistus II (1119–1124)
163. Honorius II (1124–1130)
164. Innocent II (1130–1143)
165. Celestine II (1143–1144)
166. Lucius II (1144–1155)
167. Bl. Eugene III (1145–1153)
168. Anastasius IV (1153–1154)
169. Adrian IV (1154–1159)
170. Alexander III (1159–1181)
171. Lucius III (1181–1185)
172. Urban III (1185–1187)
173. Gregory VIII (1187)
174. Clement III (1187–1191)
175. Celestine III (1191–1198)
176. Innocent III (1198–1216)
177. Honorius III (1216–1227)
178. Gregory IX (1227–1241)
179. Celestine IV (1241)
180. Innocent IV (1243–1254)
181. Alexander IV (1254–1261)
182. Urban IV (1261–1264)
183. Clement IV (1265–1268)
184. Bl. Gregory X (1271–1276)
185. Bl. Innocent V (1276)
186. Adrian V (1276)
187. John XXI (1276–1277)
188. Nicholas III (1277–1280)
189. Martin IV (1281–1285)
190. Honorius IV (1285–1287)
191. Nicholas IV (1288–1292)
192. St. Celestine V (1294)
193. Boniface VIII (1294–1303)
194. Bl. Benedict XI (1303–1304)
195. Clement V (1305–1314)
196. John XXII (1316–1334)
197. Benedict XII (1334–1342)
198. Clement VI (1342–1352)
199. Innocent VI (1352–1362)
200. Bl. Urban V (1362–1370)
201. Gregory XI (1370–1378)
202. Urban VI (1378–1389)

203. Boniface IX (1389–1404)
204. Innocent VII (1404–1406)
205. Gregory XII (1406–1415)
206. Martin V (1417–1431)
207. Eugene IV (1431–1447)
208. Nicholas V (1447–1455)
209. Callistus III (1455–1458)
210. Pius II (1458–1464)
211. Paul II (1464–1471)
212. Sixtus IV (1471–1484)
213. Innocent VIII (1484–1492)
214. Alexander VI (1492–1503)
215. Pius III (1503)
216. Julius II (1503–1513)
217. Leo X (1513–1521)
218. Adrian VI (1522–1523)
219. Clement VII (1523–1534)
220. Paul III (1534–1549)
221. Julius III (1550–1555)
222. Marcellus II (1555)
223. Paul IV (1555–1559)
224. Pius IV (1559–1565)
225. St. Pius V (1566–1572)
226. Gregory XIII (1572–1585)
227. Sixtus V (1585–1590)
228. Urban VII (1590)
229. Gregory XIV (1590–1591)
230. Innocent IX (1591)
231. Clement VIII (1592–1605)
232. Leo XI (1605)
233. Paul V (1605–1621)
234. Gregory XV (1621–1623)
235. Urban VIII (1623–1644)
236. Innocent X (1644–1655)
237. Alexander VII (1655–1667)
238. Clement IX (1667–1669)
239. Clement X (1670–1676)
240. Bl. Innocent XI (1676–1689)
241. Alexander VIII (1689–1691)
242. Innocent XII (1691–1700)
243. Clement XI (1700–1721)
244. Innocent XIII (1721–1724)
245. Benedict XIII (1724–1730)
246. Clement XII (1730–1740)
247. Benedict XIV (1740–1758)
248. Clement XIII (1758–1769)
249. Clement XIV (1769–1774)
250. Pius VI (1775–1799)
251. Pius VII (1800–1823)
252. Leo XII (1823–1829)
253. Pius VIII (1829–1830)
254. Gregory XVI (1831–1846)
255. Bl. Pius IX (1846–1878)
256. Leo XIII (1878–1903)
257. St. Pius X (1903–1914)
258. Benedict XV (1914–1922)
259. Pius XI (1922–1939)
260. Pius XII (1939–1958)
261. Bl. John XXIII (1958–1963)
262. Paul VI (1963–1978)
263. John Paul I (1978)
264. John Paul II (1978–2005)
265. Benedict XVI (2005–2013)
266. Francis (2013–)

Scripture and Tradition on the Papacy

A Man Called Simon—Matthew 4:18-20; John 1:42; Genesis 17:1-8; 17:15-16

Simon on the Sea—Matthew 14:22-33

Simon the Rock—Matthew 16:13-18

The Keys of the Kingdom—Matthew 16:19; Isaiah 22:19-23; Revelation 3:7; Saint Augustine, *Letters*, no. 53.

The Last Supper— Matthew 26:26-29; Mark14:22-25; Luke 22:14-20.

Cock Crows—Matthew 26:69-75; Mark 14:66-72; Luke 22:54-62; John 18:15-18, 25-27

Feed My Lambs—John 10:1-30; 21:1-23; Psalm 100

The First Pope—Acts 2:1-42; 9:32-35; 12:1-19

The Chair of Saint Peter—Matthew 23:1-3; Acts 1:15-26, 15:1-12; Exodus 18:13-16; Saint Macarius of Egypt, *Homily*, no. 26

Saint Peter's Crucifixion—John 21:18-19; 2 Peter 1:13-15; St. Jerome, *De Viris Illustribus*, 1, 5

Four Great Popes

   Clement I—Philippians 4:3; St. Clement of Rome, Letter to the Corinthians

   Leo the Great—Council of Chalcedon (451 a.d.)

   Pius X (the Tenth)—Matthew 19:14

   John Paul II—Matthew 14:27; Mark 6:50; Luke 5:10; John 6:20

What Does the Pope Do Today?— Luke 22:31-32; John 10:16; 1 Peter; 2 Peter; First Vatican Council, *Pastor Aeternus*, 4

Where Does the Pope Live?—1 Peter 5:12-14; St. Irenaeus, *Against Heresies*, Book III,1,1

Who Are the Pope's Helpers?—Acts 6:1-6; Saint Clement of Rome, *Letter to the Corinthians*, 65

How Is a New Pope Chosen?—Acts 1:15-26; 1 Timothy 3:1-7

Pray for the Holy Father—Acts 12:5; St. Jerome, Commentaries on Twelve of David's Psalms, 40:30

Printed by Donnelley, Mexico
Printed on October, 2013
Job Number MGN 13017
Printed in compliance with the Consumer Protection Safety Act, 2008.